The 40 Day Sadhana Companion
A Guided Journal

by Kathe Forrest

*Maybe you are searching among branches for
what only appears in the roots.*   *–Rumi*

Unique Press
Eugene, Oregon

Copyright 2013 © Kathe Forrest
AKA Siri Kirin Kaur
Illustrations by Jeshua Gideon Forrest
Edited by Susie Hairston
Back cover photo by Stephen Franzen

All teachings, yoga sets, techniques, kriyas and meditations courtesy of The Teachings of Yogi Bhajan. Reprinted with permission. Unauthorized duplication is a violation of applicable laws. ALL RIGHTS RESERVED. No part of these Teachings may be reproduced or transmitted in any form by any means, electronic or mechanical, including photocopying and recording, or by any information storage and retrieval system, except as may be expressly permitted in writing by The Teachings of Yogi Bhajan. To request permission, please write to KRI at PO Box 1819, Santa Cruz, NM 87567 or see www.kriteachings.org.

Medical disclaimer: This information is not meant to replace medical treatment where indicated. Results may vary. Please consult your physician before starting any new physical exercise program.

The 40 Day Sadhana Companion (formerly *Keep the Change*)

Acknowledgements

Thanks, first and foremost, go to my editor, Susie Hairston, who is intelligent, creative and compassionate, understanding and kind. I now understand more concretely why and how editors do their job after witnessing Susie use her gifts of accuracy, connecting sentences, adding here, adding there for better flow, and on and on. I honestly could not have succeeded without her guidance! Most of all, I thank her for time invested in this book when she continued her busy life of teaching and being a mom. Your caring spirit and passionate attitude made all the difference.

I also wish to express deep gratitude to Siri Neel Kaur Khalsa at KRI for her endless patience, sensitivity and words of wisdom. Thank you to Mehtab Benton for 40 Ways to Do 40 Days and to Derek Amarpreet Whitman for his essay on keeping a yoga journal.

To my family, Cesa, Jeremiah and Jeshua for their support and to all who contributed stories, conversations, thoughts on the title, encouragement and assistance, Many, Many thanks!

Table of Contents

Preface i

Introduction v

Chapter 1 Sadhana and the 40 Days Experience 1

Chapter 2 Others' Experiences with Meditation 11

Chapter 3 Meditations and Yoga Exercises 29

Chapter 4 Your Own Experience! Journal Pages 39

Chapter 5 What to Do After 40 Days 93

Chapter 6 Pitfalls and Tips 97

Appendix A: Chakras 105

Appendix B: Explanation of Meditation Durations 109

Appendix C: Where to find instructions for meditations ... 113

Appendix D: Resources 117

Works Cited 121

About the Author 123

Preface

"Perceive, then conceive, then deliver, then nurse and then experience. This is the concept of prayer."
−Yogi Bhajan (7-19-82)

The idea for this journal came during a meditation in December of 2011. I was in the middle of a 40-day yogic practice when I thought how nice it would be to have a place to write and document my spiritual rituals (feelings, thoughts, details of meditation, yoga exercises) instead of always writing in my day-to-day journal. It would be much easier to reference what I had done if I could go to a diary that documented only my meditative work rather than searching through an all-encompassing journal. I realized also that I could have used something like this to understand more fully the theory and concept of a continual practice during my Kundalini yoga training.

I contemplated, if this would be helpful and practical for me, it would also be useful for yogis or yoga students or anyone engaged in some type of spiritual practice on a daily basis who, like me, had been recording their experience somewhere else. At the very least they would have an efficient tool to use.

The word or phrase "Keep Up" is used during a yoga class to encourage you to keep going, to do the best that you can and to be happy about that degree of effort. This journal helps you "keep up."

I myself enjoy discipline and organization; the two fit together well for me. They might for others also.

As Kundalini yoga master Yogi Bhajan so wisely tell us, "Everybody has God's light and it must be lit by a person's own discipline. And the glass to keep it lit and shining should be kept by the person's own courage, strength and grit" (lecture, 7/26/90).

How can this book help me?
Why would you read this book?

One: you will learn how to overcome obstacles, which beset each one of us and often appear as we begin a challenge of any kind, let alone one that lasts 40 days. Your mind will begin to quiet and clear after siting for a period of time, especially if you continue this practice daily, establishing a regular rhythm. Gradually, from within, you will gain the motivation to be self-aware.

Two: You will come to a clearer understanding of sadhana, a daily spiritual practice that can lead to breakthroughs in all areas of your life. I will give you individual examples of 40 day and longer sadhanas in order to demystify this yogic practice and make it accessible to everyone.

Three: You will, I believe, be motivated by the personal stories of those who have gone before you. These inspirational tales will encourage you to keep going! To keep up!

Four: It is my hope that, ultimately, this book will make it possible for you to cultivate the neutral or meditative mind, thus improving your self-esteem and self-image by assisting you to stay focused, follow through, and remain consistent.

Introduction

This is about journaling and documenting your spiritual discipline and progression for reference. It's a step-by-step monitoring of that process, of what happens inwardly and outwardly, and the struggles and the joys of a day-by-day routine in touch with your highest Self! This focus allows you to compare current actions with your "truth" or internal standards and beliefs.

Anyone can benefit from the change brought about over 40 or 90 days or longer by simply engaging in a practice and recording his or her experiences. This will lead to one pointed focus, called Dharana (meaning "steadfastness" in Sanskrit), and the ability to be present.

Consistency is the key here—training the mind everyday with yoga, reflecting in a personal journal and reminding yourself of what can be and what is—the present moment. The neutral mind is a balanced mind—a mind that can remain calm in storms—be they emotional or physical.

How this works

Chapter 1 explains sadhana and the 40 days experience—what it does, how it works, and the history and benefits of its practice in many traditions. **Chapter 2** gives examples of people's genuine experiences using this technology* and their reflections on their yogic practices.

Chapter 3 describes in detail meditations and yogic practices to choose from. **Chapter 4** is your journaling space—the most juicy and relevant feature—*Your own Experience*!

Chapter 5 deals with what to do after the 40 days, and **Chapter 6** prepares you for pitfalls and provides tips to help keep you on your path.

Appendix A explains chakras. **Appendix B** explains the rationale behind meditating for a certain number of days and the rationale for the duration of each meditation session. **Appendix C** lists places you can find instructions for other meditations mentioned, but not explicitly described, in this book. **Appendix D** provides resources for further exploration of kriyas and meditations, as well as other useful information.

---

*The word technology is used in Kundalini yoga to mean a method (such as meditation, mantra, or asana) used to achieve your spiritual goals. The words "tools" and "tool bag" are also used in this context.

Sadhana and the 40 Day Experience

*"Doing anything for 40 days or longer provides
you the experience of discipline and teaches you
that you can go through obstacles in life and create
the change you desire."*
–Yogi Bhajan

Let me first explain what sadhana can be for you. Sadhana is a daily practice an individual performs to assist with a spiritual path. In this book I will interchange the term "sadhana" with "40-day practice," as the latter is a conscious decision to perform sadhana with a specific intention. You can benefit from sadhana whether you are affiliated with a particular religion or not. Sadhana encourages discipline, which is at the very core of yogic philosophy. It is a long-lived tradition and one of the four steps as described in the Yogic sutra—"Sadhana Pada," which refers to discipline and practices such as meditation, hatha yoga, physical exercise and channeling the emotions. Direct cultivation of personal experience and capacity enables a person to uplift him or herself and expand his or her awareness.

Sadhana is a structure in which anyone can develop skills to cultivate self-awareness.

Yogi Bhajan, Master of Kundalini yoga explains in the Kundalini Yoga Teacher Training manual that discipline in turn leads to commitment, which leads to character. "Character is when all your characteristics—all facets, flaws, and facts about yourself are under control and in balance" (The Aquarian teacher 9).

A good way to develop discipline and get into a positive routine is to start with a **40-day practice**. A life-promoting habit is a daily one. It takes a certain mindset to change ingrained patterns.

It takes 40 days to change a habit.

What does that mean?
Obviously, the more time you devote to an undertaking, the more you will reap from it.

But why 40 days?
Guru Singh from Los Angeles, who teaches at the Yoga West Studio, explains the importance of 40 days from a biochemical standpoint; as he explains, our body's blood cells contain iron. Iron is a metal that we use to record on such devices as tape recorders and cassettes, and the original magnetic tape in a tape recorder was ferric-oxide tape.

2.4 million new erythrocites or red blood cells are produced in the body every second. These cells are made in the bone marrow and circulate for about 100–120 days before they are recycled. As they are made and circulate, they store information and record our attitudes (about who we are at that moment). So, as you can see, after 40 days, new blood cells imprinted with the new thought/mantra/intention that we have been meditating on for 40–120 days are beginning to outnumber the old ones. Performing the practice for 40 days allows the meditation to release any thought patterns that hinder us.

That is why it takes 40 days to really begin to create or revise a habit, and, if you continue to do the meditation or practice for 120 days, the habit becomes you. Some psychologists suggest that over 90 percent of what we do everyday derives from our habits. From the way we brush our teeth, to the way we eat our dinner, including the activities we perform after we finish our dinner.

In addition to the biochemical and psychological reasons for undertaking a 40-day practice, there are many historical precedents for undertaking spiritual journeys/challenges for 40 days, as the number 40 plays a significant role in many religious traditions and spiritual journeys.

In the Islamic faith—the number 40 is repeated many times. Muhammad was praying and fasting in a cave for *40 days* and had *40 followers* to spread the religion of Islam. Regarding the flood that Noah encountered, it is said that for *forty days* water continued to pour from the heavens and to stream out over the earth. And the Koran contains the following description of a 40-day devotion to and immersion in Allah that reads as if it were a description of the benefits of performing a sadhana today: *"Believers have also been encouraged to devote themselves to Source for forty days to see the springs of wisdom break forth from their hearts and flow from their tongues" ("The Significance of the Number 40 in Islam").*

In the Jewish tradition, it is well known that *prayers said for 40 consecutive days* have great power. Furthermore, these prayers are even more powerful when they take place at the *Western Wall*, considered by many to be the holiest place on earth, where, according to Jewish belief, prayers from all over the world gather to ascend to Heaven. There are many stories of people whose prayers were miraculously answered and whose lives were dramatically changed after the completion of 40 days of prayer at the Western Wall.

This total commitment, combined with the fact that a person is willing to clear his schedule every day, for *40 consecutive days*, in order to focus on prayers and his relationship with Spirit, is probably part of the secret of why this spiritual ritual is, in fact, a success.

The Christian faith has many examples of individuals undertaking spiritual journeys for 40 days, such as Moses on the mountain asking forgiveness for 40 days and Jesus fasting in the desert for *40 days*. Additionally, the number *forty* represents preparation, penance and purification. The Lenten fast in preparation for Easter lasts *forty days*.

In the Kundalini yogic system, the purpose of doing a kriya or set of yoga exercises and/or a meditation or mantra for a number of days is to precipitate discovery and instigate **change.** "Kriya" means an action for manifestation.

"We practice 40-day meditations to embody new experiences or increased capacities. We practice 90-day meditations to clear our subconscious and build new habits. We practice 120-day meditations to realize that awareness in our daily lives. But when we want to experience self-mastery and confirm our consciousness, beyond every change of time, space and circumstance, we practice 1000 days" (G. Khalsa).

The rationale for following a practice for a certain length of time is that by doing so you connect to your intention consciously and with focus. This book will help with that in many ways. You will record the *experiences, challenges* and *changes* that happen during the 40, 90 or 120 days identified in *The Aquarian Teacher* as being particularly meaningful periods for following a practice (136). This will give you a clearer understanding of your transformation.

"Doing anything for 40 days or longer provides you the experience of discipline and teaches you that you can go through obstacles in life and create the change you desire. The duration of 40 days of practice is chosen to let the meditation provoke your subconscious to release any thoughts and emotional patterns that hinder you" (Bhajan and Singh 140).

Let's take an example:

What if you pray for prosperity? Will 40 days bestow wealth and cash?

Actually, I thought that it was possible to acquire more money in the early days of my studies of Kundalini Yoga. I even found when completing 40 days of the Har Har chant for prosperity that I did generate more money and increase my income significantly for a few weeks. However, focusing on cash as my marker for prosperity did not have the same effect as I continued the mantra.

I searched more deeply into the question of what happens when one undertakes such a lengthy commitment to either a meditation or a yoga exercise by reading and asking others in my discipline who had much more experience and practice with using these techniques than I did. Is it possible, I wondered, to effect a deep change within oneself? Could I find the root and plant a yogic seed?

In the process of this exploration, I examined the meaning of the word "change" and found that its definition describes perfectly the wealth of advantages that come with consistently cultivating positive actions daily.

An online dictionary defines change: "To make the form, nature, content, future course, etc., of (something) *different* from what it is or from what it would be if left alone" ("change," dictionary.com).

Let's examine each part of the above definition in order to understand how change relates to the practice of sadhana.

***Form*–**this suggests a structure or an appearance, and that may be what you are after—an alteration in your physical body or in how you feel about it. After doing 40 days of a meditation for the 3rd chakra or navel kriya (i.e. Stretch Pose, Sat Kriya—see Appendix C for a reference that will explain how to do this pose), you might find that in addition to having more energy, control over your body, and coordination, all the internal organs of your body are functioning better. The possibility of being able to shape and direct your life may begin.

***Nature*–**Here I want to refer to the "essential qualities, innate disposition" of a person. A 40-day commitment establishes character, leading you to dignity, then to divinity and, finally, to grace. People begin to trust you and respect you. Your temperament and behavior become attuned to all that surrounds your life and experiences (*The Aquarian Teacher 9*). Try "For a New Energy Balance" on page 110 in Shakta Kaur Khalsa's *Kundalini Yoga*, or, simply keep promises that you have made for 40 days!

***Future course*–**Now, this is exciting!! Can you change a future course?

> "Oh my soul, you come and you go
> Through the paths of time and space.
> In useless play you'll not find the way
> So set your course and go"(*Kaur et al*).

Ah! The shabds or chants are a perfect example of being able to give direction to the many aspects of the self, to redirect your future course.

"Japji", a universal song of God composed by Guru Nanak Dev, the founder of the Sikh faith, is a poem that expresses the beauty of the Universe. There are 40 verses, and each one works on a particular facet of your being. The 38th is said to give you the power to rewrite your own destiny. These simple and sweet words said 11X/ day for 40–1000 days will help move the energy in your aura and, therefore, your surroundings, to supersede any future course towards which you were headed at that moment.

The second meaning of change in the online dictionary is:

To transform–You can alter a behavior with discipline!

Kriya to Relieve Inner Anger is a perfect example of this idea. Here is a set of movements that is directed at getting rid of the emotions that are interfering with your relationships with others by removing the pent up rage and irritation that is blocking your relationship with yourself and causing you to exude angry energy. This set ends with the powerful Sat Kriya moving the energy up and through the chakras while integrating all.

Another part of the definition of change is:

To substitute another or others for: exchange for something else–this builds upon the previous definition, affirming that there is an avenue to remove or replace a thought or behavior. Earlier, I mentioned the Har Har chant and the movement used in this prosperity exercise. "Har" means to create, and hitting the sides of the hands when saying "Har", activates the meridians in the body for accessing brain power, and will thus generate new thoughts and ideas to bring you the "green stuff" or help to clarify ideas about what prosperity means to you.

During your 40 days, altering attitudes is possible: "I am so poor" can be replaced with, "I am blessed and prospering through the Divinity within me." Change can indicate a little or a lot, right? You can modify or adjust something as much as is necessary. You will be the judge of that as you work your way through and into this astonishing experience!

As you begin your own practice, it is important to recognize that even something as small as changing the word you use to describe or think about something can make a profound difference.

One of the 5 guiding principles of Unity* is that what we think, feel, and believe creates our experience of our world. This belief is prevalent across the globe. It is not uncommon to hear it spoken of on the news, in a church, at a gathering, or as a topic of discussion on Oprah. The idea that what we speak and imagine, whether it be positive or negative, heavily influences our life is becoming a Guide for the planet.

Before you speak, THINK

Is it necessary?

Is it true?

Is it kind?

Will it hurt anyone?

Will it improve on the silence?

---

*A spiritual path awakening us to and allowing us to experience our Authentic Eternal Self and the presence and power of the infinite Spirit in all life (Unity of the Valley website).

Carry this philosophy one step further and immerse yourself in a spiritual practice (40–120 days) where you continually think, feel and believe that what you are doing makes a subtle change. Then, your sensitivity to and intuition about the world around you will increase.

Before moving on, I will leave you with a thought. Everyone will have a different experience. That's the beauty of it. For just 7 days complete something that you've wanted to improve in your life, that you've attempted before and not been able to finish. See how that feels to you. Gradually increase until you arrive at 40 days. It's a difficult task, but well worth the process. Believe in yourself, and hold to your intention. Also, don't expect! Allow! Be present without judgment.

It is important to note that these changes will continue even if you stop at 40 days. This is a subtle process and a great way to stay focused.

My best wish for you is that the Pure Light within you guide your way on...

Sat Nam

Namaste

How to choose a meditation: A look at others' experiences with meditation

*"The inspiration you seek is
already within you."*
—Rumi

Before you read about others' intimate practices, I need to say a few words regarding starting a spiritual practice and what to choose. If this is your first time, and you know what you want to do—Go for It! But…if you are unsure, think about what is happening in your life right now.

Are you happy and satisfied with a relationship you are in, or could it be better? Would you like deeper connections in your friendships? How is your physical body? Or your mental state?

Is there an annoying habit that you would like to get rid of? Find an area of your life that you would like to focus on and choose a practice that will allow you to work on that area.

For example, perhaps you are feeling that your friends don't call you on a regular basis to check in or get together with you, or maybe you want more intimacy with new friends, a closer connection. Take the 40 days to improve the relationships you have by examining your interactions with your friends. Are there patterns to change here? Do you reply fully to emails sent to you? Do you call your friends and ask if they would like to talk over breakfast or a walk? Are you writing letters to those you love, but who live in another state or country? Taking a full six weeks to focus on this area of your life will allow you to fully and deeply examine what your true intention is and how you wish to transform some tendency within yourself that could be holding you back from either making a commitment to yourself or a necessary alteration in your thought process, speech or behavior.

As you read the following testimonies, allow the words to wash in and around you. But—and I would like to emphasize—this is your journey, and a simple pranayama (breathing) exercise may be just the right one; or if you want to start something more complex, but the recommended time seems too much, you could begin with 3 minutes and then increase the time as you get more comfortable. I share the experiences below to inspire you, not to make you feel that one person's practice is better than another's or that you must follow a certain practice in order to achieve your goals. Know now, that whatever you choose after reading these accounts, the spiritual journey you are about to begin is for you and only you, the Soul within. Instructions are not given for the meditations described below, so if you would like to try any of them, please see Appendix C, which lists sites and books where specific instructions for these meditations can be found.

The Experience
On deciding what meditation to do: "Choosing something to begin with needs to be an organic process. Today I began the Sat Kriya

meditation simply because it came to me while I sat meditating. Other times I have had to look through my yoga books for a reminder of what is out there to immerse myself in. Or I have chosen a kriya because of something going on in my life that I thought would help a family member or myself. I have done the So Purkh meditation and did notice improvements in relationships."

These words from my friend and fellow teacher Charinbir about sum it up in a nutshell. In some teacher trainings, you are told what meditation to begin with, and in others, you pick whichever one you would like to use.*

On practicing So Purkh, a meditation that helps women to feel whole and balanced: Yogi Bhajan spoke glowingly about the tremendous power and potential of reciting SO PURKH. He said a woman could use this shabd to beam on a man to:

Attract a child to you who will become a man of God

Heal a man

Transform a man into a man of God

Attract a man of God to be your husband

Make God appear before you

A young woman I know shared her experience with, and feelings about the So Purkh meditation:

---

*And if you are not in a teacher training, but want to begin, I have included resources in this book to help your journey.

I started a daily So Purkh practice last July for various reasons—the sheer beauty of it, wanting to attract a spiritual partner, blessing and cutting ties with past partners, but mostly to "make God appear before me", which is the one description of this shabd that is not male-centric. One thing I've been experiencing is that this Shabd, for me, grounds me in my identity as a woman as I relate to men. I feel this shabd fulfills the longing for God that we as woman tend to channel into desire for a partner. I experience a peace that God is with me and supports me from inside my being. I find it reconditions the idea we see in popular culture that soul fulfillment is found through relationships, and reconnects us to the knowledge that it is found in our relationship with God/our soul. It's important for women to connect to that male-God polarity within so we don't feel like we need to go outside of ourselves to get it. My feelings are that this inner landscape of peace in women is needed in order for us to have a balanced intimate relationship with a man. And also, that if it's not in our cards to be in a relationship, we are whole and happy anyway. How blessed we are to have this practice as women! But that's my experience as a young single woman. And it's been a gradual opening for me.

On practicing a 90-day So Purkh meditation as experienced by Jennifer Marcaccini: My experience: I committed to this meditation as part of my authentic relationship course. I had found the man who would be my husband, but I thought he needed a little spiritual help and guidance to fully realize this. I also wanted to clear all past relationships from my arc line. I recited the meditation for 31 minutes each day or 11 times throughout the day. I felt very connected and felt my strength as a woman when I was chanting this meditation. Throughout the 90 days I also noticed my soon-to-be husband transforming and becoming much stronger, clearer and connected to all that is. As time went on we solidified our relationship—moving from friends to an intimate partnership, which culminated with me moving in with him after relocating to California. 20 months later we are married and pregnant with our first child. It is a powerful meditation that strengthens a woman to hold space for the man or soon-to-be man in her life.

On practicing extended Kundalini Meditations as experienced by David Barfoot 4/21/12: My first experience with extended meditation was with Burn Inner Anger. I did 40 days with one arm extended, 40 days with the other arm and 40 more days with both arms extended. It was physically and emotionally very challenging. The arms ached severely in the first several days and then gradually acclimated. The pain, combined with the required strong, powerful breath (and whatever forces unknown to me) provoked unexpected bursts of tears, screaming and howlings of rage and grief. What I felt was as much about grief (perhaps more so) than anger. I should explain that my wife had recently left me, and I began this meditation in an effort to handle my feelings. The experience helped, but it did not miraculously cure my anger issues, nor did it change my circumstances from which much of the anger originated. I still had much inner work to do (practicing new ways of dealing with frustration) and much work rearranging my outer world.

My Level I teacher training required 40 days each of 7, 11, and 31 minute meditations respectively. My 7-minute one was Meditation for Projection & Protection for the Heart. The 11-minute one was Guru Ram Das Meditation. The 31-minute one was Indra Nittri Meditation. I did all three concurrently. It's hard to break down what each one did. With all, as with the Burn Inner Anger, there was a progression of focus and expertise. It seemed that I would keep experiencing new levels of performance. Every time I thought I had it down, I would go to a different level of perfection. Much was happening and transforming inside me at this time with the teacher training and these meditations. Things were moving fast inside and out, and the meditations were part of it all. All I can say is they kept me high but also centered as my inner and outer world changed. When doing extended meditations, I reach a place where I look forward to and depend on them. I feel good doing them and after doing them. I would not feel good if I missed a day. I gradually worked up my time doing Sat Kriya from 3 minutes to 31 minutes. I did a very slow progression over a period of about 3 months, as the instructions warned against jumping into 31 minutes too suddenly. I then began doing a 31 minute Sat Kriya every day. I'm embarrassed to say I forgot how long I did it. I think for about 90 days. I would feel so good afterwards that I looked forward to it. It kept me centered, and I felt like it transmuted and moved my sexual energies upward. It did not reduce my sexual feelings but somehow helped in dealing with a non-active sex life.

I am currently doing 90 days of Meditation to Break the Mask. I missed my 33rd day and resumed the following day. I have done another 32 days since then. This was the very first time I've ever missed a day with any of my extended meditations. Not a good feeling. This is by far the most difficult meditation I've ever done. It requires inhaling 1/3, holding for 15 seconds, inhaling 2/3, holding for 15 seconds, then inhaling fully and holding another 15 seconds, exhaling and repeating for 15 minutes followed by 11 minutes of out loud mantra (harjee har har har har harjee), followed by another 5 minutes of the first exercise. For the first 30 or 40 days, it required incredible self-control for me not to panic and gasp for air. I would break into a sweat every time. Now (knock on wood) the body and mind seem to be adjusting so that I forget where I am in the progression, and I must focus to stay present (Much to my relief!). Learning to stay present is inherent in all meditations. An article in *Scientific American* on holding the breath dispelled any fear I had that harm would come to my brain during this extreme exercise. This meditation is a requirement for a Level II teacher training in Conscious Communication. So, this meditation, along with my other work in this course is definitely bringing me to a more authentic place with greater presence in my interactions with others. Things seem to spill easily from my mouth in a truthful but non-offensive way. Compassion is very present. It has helped in my teaching of Kundalini by helping to keep me in teacher mode with less of my ego identity in the way. I like myself better and am happier. Wahe Guru!

–from David Barfoot or Charinbir

On practicing Meditation to Tap Opportunities as experienced by Siri Kirin: I started this prosperity meditation by reciting Hariang (Ha ree ong) 16X on one breath for 11 minutes. I increased to 22 minutes and continued until I had done it for 40 days. I then increased every day until I reached 31 minutes and held there until 90 days. I ended up doing this for 120 days.

I love saying Hariang. The recitation takes me into the "zone". I have seen results too. Hariang means to destroy, and my intention in using it has been to get rid of all that hampers or impedes my success. That has included up to today—money worries, work, the idea of lack, the feeling of not being empowered. I feel light in my being and sure don't want to stop.

For me—these happenings are both subtle and remarkable.

Along with Hariang I did a 4th chakra kriya, sometimes known as Green energy kriya. This was more challenging, as it was a physical set of yoga postures, some of which I did not resonate with; however, I did 40 days. On the 3rd day into it, I had received a needed $300, and on the 10th day, I had attracted more students to my yoga classes. I also had the seed thought for this book, and during this time, ideas came and fell away. I realize, as I go back to my specific 40-day journal, how the time spent on those meditations helped me to overcome the many, many challenges that came my way and enabled me to get through them all. I was telling a friend today, thinking of life as a winding path works for me; we meander or run this way and that, and then, when we stop and look back over several months, we realize oh! That's what that was about! Aha!

On the benefits of a steadfast commitment to a spiritual practice as shared by Emily Hine: As Rumi said, "What nine months does for the embryo, forty early mornings will do for your growing awareness."

Yesterday I completed my commitment to forty days of consecutive meditation and yoga. I was inspired by a woman from Boise Idaho, who started Winter Feast for the Soul. I wanted to jump-start my spiritual practice, and I knew I would have a higher success rate if I joined 10,000 other people around the world who had also made the commitment. I threw yoga in for "fun". I thought—how hard could it possibly be to get really conscious every day? I posted my goal on my facebook page for accountability and support.

The type of meditation I practice is called Vipassana, which is a fancy word for mindfulness meditation. This is essentially the practice of being an observer of yourself, your mind and your actions without judgment, but with complete neutrality and acceptance. The type of yoga I do is typically Bikram Yoga: 26 poses in a room heated to over 100 degrees. Think Gumby in a lulu lemon outfit!

I don't own a television and pride myself on not putting junk into my body or mind (all that often, anyway.) However, this 40-day commitment to mindfulness pushed every resistance button in my body. I realized on day 3 how much the monkey-mind/ego takes over directing thoughts, and kept me from just being neutral. Complete stories will be crafted by the mind if left un-checked. So, I checked mine into a mental hospital! Actually, I asked for help. I prayed (more like begged) for neutrality and a peaceful mind. One fine morning, it actually happened, complete bliss. No thoughts, no judgments, just bliss for a very few precious moments.

Thank God, literally, because after being out of practice for a while, I needed to know it was possible again. I needed a sign.

In the 40-day window, some extraordinary things (not all good) happened.

Letting go of attachment: First of all, I decided to put my beautiful floating home on the market. It had been a wonderful place to call home in Seattle, but it felt like a skin I'd outgrown after occupying it for 12 years. I felt like it no longer gave me room to grow and, therefore, might actually be holding me back. This was not a new thought; it just persisted more this time (perhaps because I was meditating every day, giving those thoughts room to expand and direct my spirit).

Instead of preparing my house to sell, I prepared my house for the next owner. It was a subtle, but important distinction. I took care to enhance the nurturing qualities of the home and fix what I could. I hoped that a potential new owner would feel how the houseboat literally hugs you when you walk in the door. It's a sanctuary in the city and I've always loved it here. With the conscious choice to let go, the house went on the market on February 19th. I received a full price offer on February 20th. Yes, in one day and in this economy (2010). The power of intention and attention was palpable. The woman who purchased my home was exactly my age and fell in love with it, just as I did 12 years prior. It felt good handing the baton of responsibility for this sanctuary over to her to cherish for as long as she needs it.

Saying goodbye: The second thing that happened was a terrible tragedy among our floating home community. We lost a dear friend and her 3-month old baby, both within a 12-hour period. There still aren't words to describe the emotional loss that all of us feel. The only "good" that can be found in a situation like this was the community that stepped forward to help those left behind. Hearts emerged to start the grieving; hands emerged to get things done. Time to heal is all that we have left.

Added to these physical and emotional transitions were all the earthquakes and unhealthy healthcare debates, and a general state of global unrest. I wanted desperately to abandon my commitment to daily meditation and yoga, and I certainly had good excuses that anyone would understand. But, I stopped to think about that. What is it in us that wants to go unconscious when things get painful? Why is it we want to unplug, numb out and eat poorly when it's the most important time of all to be conscious, feel the pain, and share our common humanity? I know intellectually that if I feel it, it will pass through me like a cloud passing overhead. It will revisit, but each time it won't stay quite as long. I know this intellectually, but what kept me going was the emotional support from my friends on Facebook, my accountability team who said "you can do it" even when I didn't think I could, or more accurately, when I just didn't want to. I would walk into meetings at work, and people following my status updates would say, "It's day 18 today, isn't it? How's it going?" Wow. People were paying attention and cared about my progress. It inspired them to start their own program and gave them confidence that they could, so I couldn't possibly quit.

Each day that I kept doing yoga and meditation felt like I was making a statement that "no, I will not go unconscious." Too many people are unconscious, which is why we have such a mess to clean up in our country. Sometimes I cried in the middle of yoga, grieving for my lost friend and her husband left behind. Some days, after yoga and meditation, I allowed myself to go unconscious. I started watching episodes of *Grey's Anatomy* and *Desperate Housewives* (gasp!) at night while I carbo-loaded on cereal. I had to be okay with allowing this, resist the judgment, but keep the awareness. This is not WHO I am. This is WHAT I'm doing, in this moment, to avoid feeling. The avoidance of pain and conflict is a primal instinct, and sometimes we just have to let the primate win. And then begin again tomorrow, hoping the adult, wise, emotionally intelligent self will be back in the driver's seat.

At the end of the experiment, I meditated 39 days out of 40. It's actually good I didn't complete all 40 days. It keeps my "perfectionista" in check. She's based in ego, but my soul is driving the bus now, thank you very much. Her fuel is daily meditation, writing, yoga, emotional connection with friends when we are in pain and when we aren't. She's fed by doing work that matters in the world, expansion, expression, letting go of the old even if it's uncomfortable. She heals by feeling the deep, incredible loss of a friend and then moving forward even when momentum feels nearly impossible.

Going unconscious is easy; we have created a world of consumption that has dumbed us down and numbed us out. Doing the work to stay awake and emotionally connected in this world is hard, especially when there is so much tragedy and so many distractions, but that's what we are here to do, and we are so much stronger when we do it in community.

With love and respect to those in transition, and those learning to hear and honor their souls, and with gratitude to Facebook, the surprising source of support I received literally and virtually every day. (Emily Hine's experience first appeared on her website HineSights.)

On performing a 40-day sadhana while recuperating from a grave illness as shared by Guruatma: After an extended period of chemotherapy (5 yrs), high-dosage prednisone (11 yrs) and taking many (about 20) other Rx drugs, my nervous system was shot - I WAS A WRECK and felt like a walking, open wound still fighting on the war front. Even though I thought I was insane to do it, because I knew I would definitely suffer to even TRY, I committed to 40 days of the 3HO Kriya to Balance and Recharge the Nervous and Immune System. It's very hard for me to hold to the discipline of 40 days. I have a 5 in my karmic position in numerology. This kriya cooled me down and definitely put me back together again - that's why I named it "Humpty Dumpty Kriya".

It was super-challenging to hold my arms up, so I started with 3 and worked my way up to 11 minutes. The end of the exercise is where you have to work the hardest; over time, I could feel things adjusting and coming into balance in my systems. This was no magic trick—I had to kick-butt and somehow, the 'umph' that I needed to do the exercises was provided, therein.

It promises to slowly and steadily build a very strong steel-like stamina in you, and that is exactly what it delivered. I extended the 40 days many times, till I felt I could afford to stop doing it. It safely brought me back into life. I really don't know what else on earth could have pulled off that miracle, and I am forever grateful for the gift of that particular yogic tool. It brought me back into life, and this is now what I coach about—what you Can Do!

Another meditation that proved to be very powerful in my life was Deep Memory of a Past Projection from The Mind book. So, here I was, brought back to life to find myself PROFOUNDLY DEAF! And no longer able to listen to music, with numb feet (peripheral neuropathy) and all kinds of other unbelievable-to-me, life-altering conditions on my plate. WHO WAS I??? If I could not be the singer and the runner and the everything-else-that-I used-to-be? All my energy was totally sucked into that irresistible memory of my past identity. Just like it (the meditation) says, I was "tempted, hypnotized and distracted" by my attachment. So…whatever is removed from your life (i.e. husband, job, hearing, etc.) and you need to know for yourself who you are now, what your focus is now—this meditation will help the past elements and past projections drop.

It was a terrible time in my life; I felt totally disoriented, desperate, depressed and REALLY MAD! I was alive but jet-lagged from life as I knew it. I seriously questioned why I was alive, and I demanded God to SHOW ME! what could possibly be the justification for hanging out on earth any longer in this condition. This meditation felt SOOOO SOOTHING to me; it has a breath pattern that I just loved doing! Thanks to repeating this meditation for many 40-day cycles, I was able to pick up and walk forward—it did the trick and I was able to drop the past, much to my surprise.

Its effects linger, even after all these years—it lives and breathes with me. Because I am late-deafened and have a memory bank of 43 years of normal hearing, when I wake up in the morning, my consciousness automatically presents with the memory of being able to HEAR, but I soon find out that I am still deaf.

This meditation is my forever-anchor—it provides me with a tool that is always 'under my belt'. It helps me absorb that waking-up shock so that I am able to move right into coaching myself, "This is who you are, today, Guruatma; you can do this and 'keep up' and be happy!"

My soul's purposeful fulfillment depends on finding this platform to perch on; it keeps me in the reality, and I get to forever practice not relating to anything that limits me.

Thank you for the opportunity to share this precious and powerful technology, Siri Kirin.

Satnaam
Guruatma K Khalsa
Yogic-tools.com

On practicing Bound Lotus, as experienced by Akal Sahai Singh: "I've been blessed to have practiced Bound Lotus every day since September14, 2005, and the experience continues to grow, continues to deepen, uplift and elevate; every single moment of every single day, I surrender, I become more, I become, myself."

On practicing a prosperity sadhana as a couple, as shared by Harsimranpreet Kaur Rai: So my husband, Manjit Singh, and I have done a couple of prosperity meditations now. The first one was the 25th pauri of Japji, "Bahota karam." This was my husband's first 40-day meditation, and he started to experience challenges within the first 10 days. He started to have to pay out money—a 1000 pound loan to his brother-in-law was the biggest, then there were special needs for airfare for a friend, and his employer did not pay him his correct wage, but instead gave him a check for well below the minimum wage. He had to fight steadily for proper pay. For him, the challenges didn't stop, and he was glad to see the meditation go.

I, however, had a different experience. People were surprising me with food and taking me out to eat! During this time, my father passed and left me money that I was able to use to pay some college loans. That was a surprise. Also, I had been searching for a job knowing that I did not want the kind of work I was applying for, and this money left me free to find my purpose.

We finished the second extended meditation about 6 weeks ago; we had started that one with the intention of having our own home. We did the third part of Kirtan Sohila: "Gagan mai thall..."[1] It's a very earthy shabd[2], and it brought so much nature and interaction with the earth

---

[1] Kirtan Sohila–Evening hymn of the prayers of the Sikhs. The hymns are meant for the whole world and are applicable to people of any nationality or religion.
[2] Shabd (sha bud)–sound current or vibration

to us, which is something I really need living in a city—walks in the park and lots of animals. While it didn't give us our own home, I started noticing around day 21 that the family home we were living in was becoming the kind of place we wanted to live in, and our discipline was settling in. There was more love and happiness; we had some kirtanees come from India and bless us with a kirtan; another visitor, a dear friend from India came and did prayers with us. Family was gathering that hadn't been. We had a few small old business items come up we needed to clear, and I received lots of little amounts of money from well-wishers and visitors. We don't always get the things we wish for, but we do get what we need.

"You can't always get what you want, but you get what you neeeeed!"

On the experience of longer meditations and prosperity as experienced by Marlene Brown: I'm on day 79 of my sadhana and before this I did 180 days of Subagh Kriya, but I cannot calculate the benefits, and I feel I am slow to learn. I want to be positive. I feel good and strong and healthy. I would like a breakthrough! I cannot seem to manifest abundance or prosperity. Maybe I have, and I just don't realize it. I love Kundalini yoga and am still waiting for what is on the other side. Waiting patiently, but waiting.

When I did a prosperity workshop with Siri Kirin in 2010, during the meditation I woke up a spirit, who ended up hiding my keys for a month. This taught me lessons in humility. I had to ask for rides to work and finally got another set of keys made for an electronic lock system. Then, I found the keys and got an unknown text with just a smiley face. It was strange but I never talked to him (Hariang) again, too mischievous.

I hope that one day I can show my family all the benefits of yoga and how strong I have become doing the yogic exercises (kriyas). I will continue to do the work and brighten the world as I go along my path.

On a person's first experience with Kundalini meditations as shared by Kim Thompson: The practice of the 40-day sadhana changed my life. For years I heard about meditation and yoga, and yet, despite my spiritual hunger, I did not feel a connection to these practices or the willingness to try. Music has always been an extremely important part of my life. Two years ago, through a weekly Internet radio program called Spirit Voyage, I was introduced to Snatam Kaur's angelic voice, the singing of mantra and Kundalini Yoga. Over the next two years of discovering and singing Kundalini music as well as Kirtan, somehow my ideas changed, and my heart opened to the practices of meditation and yoga.

In 2011 I joined Spirit Voyage and 10,000 others as we practiced my first 40-day sadhana. The kriya and mudra (hand position) were simple, the practice sat me down and taught me to breathe, and the mantra, Wahe Guru, quieted my mind and opened my heart. I continued in a personal daily practice of mantra and meditation until the next 40-day sadhana, which I joined a few months later, and have continued every day since. It has been over 10 months. Although that sounds like a short period of time, I am a different person today.

I have a connection to the Nam, the breath feeds my soul, and time in meditation each day brings me closer to Truth and Wisdom. A few months ago, I found a beginning Kundalini Yoga class, which feels like home. As a result of the practice of a 40-day sadhana, I have found within a connection to love, peace and joy. I am grateful. I AM.

Sat Nam.
Kim Thompson, AKA Namliv Kaur

How to Choose a Meditation

Onward and Upward

Now, it's your turn! The next chapter has a few meditations and sets to choose from, but there are a myriad of ways to amend one's habits.

You do not have to go by any rules.

I want this to be a place that encourages you to create seeds for change. Choose one practice and Go for It!

3
Choices of Meditations & Yoga Exercises

*The changes we are seeking can be effectively
initiated from within,
while at the same time having a powerful
external result.*

This chapter will explain a few simple Kundalini Yoga meditations and kriyas as taught by Yogi Bhajan® to help you begin the process of a 40 or 90 or 120-day journey, but feel free to do what seems best to you! The first chant that I personally fell in love with was actually Om Namo Shivaya, though there are many other beautiful chants to pick from. The chapter on Pitfalls has additional ideas.

Before beginning your practice or sharing these Kundalini yoga teachings with others, tune in with the phrase, "Ong Namo Guru Dev Namo." These sounds mean, "I bow to the divine teacher within." Repeating them promotes hope, strength and courage and begins to break old habits and initiate change in your life. Covering your head during meditation, though not required, helps to conserve and focus your energy.

I want to start with the first part of **Subagh Kriya, called Prosperity Meditation II** when done on its own. In general, many people use this meditation because it is simple, short (3 minutes) and easy to do. Siri Kirpal Kaur Khalsa says to do it 3 minutes if you are employed and longer if you are unemployed. For an extended version, called Subagh Kriya for Good Fortune, see Shakta Kaur Khalsa's book, *Kundalini Yoga*. Here is a link to a demonstration of the exercise: http://www.mrsikhnet.com/2011/01/31/mteditation-for-prosperity/

Position: Sit in Easy Pose—on the floor with your legs crossed and a straight spine (lengthen from the bottom of your spine to the crown of your head).

Elbows are by your sides; your forearms are angled up and outward with your fingers at the level of your throat.

Begin with your palms facing down.

Alternately hit the sides of your hands together. The Mercury (pinky) fingers and the Moon Mounds (located on the bottom of the palms) hit when your palms are facing up. When your hands hit facing down, the sides of the Jupiter (index) fingers touch, and your thumbs cross below the hands, with your right thumb under your left. Yogi Bhajan said that the thumbs crossing this way are the key to the meditation.

Eyes: Look at the tip of your nose, through eyes 9/10th closed.

Mantra: Chant the mantra "Har, Har" (pronounced "Hud, Hud"). Alternately strike the Moon area and the Jupiter area as you continuously chant "Har" with the tip of your tongue, pulling your navel in with each "Har." (I recommend doing this to the music "Tantric Har" by Simran Kaur, as its rhythm is perfect for keeping you focused while doing this meditation.)

This exercise works on the Pituitary, a gland that regulates metabolism.

It also, as Yogi Bhajan explains, has mental and spiritual effects, "To become rich and prosperous with wealth and values is to have the strength to come through. It means that transmissions from your brain and the power of your intuition can immediately tell you what to do. You will be in a position to change gears. If you need to go in reverse, you can go in reverse. If you need to go forward, you will go forward. This is a very old and simple system" *(June 21, 1996)*.

Meditation for a Calm Heart—Perfect for beginners

Position: Sit in Easy Pose with a straight spine. (Lengthen from the bottom of your spine to the crown of your head.)

Eyes can either be closed or looking straight ahead with eyes 1/10 open.

Mudra: Place your left hand at the Heart center (middle of the chest). Your palm is flat against your chest with your fingers pointing to the right. Your right hand is in Gyan Mudra with the tip of your index finger touching the tip of your thumb. Raise your right hand up as if taking a pledge. Your palm faces forward with the three middle fingers pointing straight up. Your forearm is perpendicular to the ground, and your elbow is relaxed near the side of your body.

Breath: Concentrate on the flow of your breath. Regulate each bit of breath consciously. Inhale slowly and deeply. Then suspend your breath and raise your chest. Retain as long as possible.

Then exhale smoothly and completely. When your breath is totally out, lock it out for as long as possible. Continue this pattern of long, deep breathing for 3–31 minutes.

To end: Inhale and exhale strongly **3 times.** Relax.

Physically, this exercise strengthens the heart and lungs. Emotionally, this breath pattern and meditation will give you a better perception of your relationships. When upset with yourself or others, sit and do this for 3 to 15 minutes before acting.

Tattva Balance Beyond Stress & Duality*
(Pranayam or breathing meditation)
The five elements (air, ether, fire, water, and earth), called tattvas, are categories of quality based in the energy flow of your life force. If all of the elements are strong, in balance, and located in their proper place in your body, then you can resist stress, trauma and illness.

Position: Sit in Easy Pose with a straight spine. Chin in, chest lifted high.

Mudra: Raise your hands in front of your heart center with your elbows bent so your forearms make a straight line parallel to the ground. Spread the fingers of both hands and press the finger and thumb tips of opposite hands together with the thumbs pointing toward your chest. Create enough pressure to join the first segments of each finger. The palms are separated.

Eyes: Fix your eyes on the tip of the nose.

Breath: Inhale smoothly and deeply through your nose. Exhale through rounded lips in 8 equal emphatic strokes, and pull your navel in on each exhale. To end, inhale deeply, exhale fully and relax.

---

* This meditation has been taken with permission and in its entirety from *The Aquarian Teacher* p. 406.

Time: Continue for three minutes. Build the practice slowly to 11 minutes.

The deep inhale gives endurance and calmness. The exhalation, through the mouth, calms reaction to stress. The strokes of the exhalation stimulate the pituitary gland to optimize your clarity, intuition and decision making capacities. This meditation resolves many inner conflicts, especially when the conflicts arise from the competition between different levels of your functioning, e.g., spiritual vs. mental vs. physical/survival needs.

Radiant Kriya images can be found at the back of the book.

Radiant Body Kriya

The Radiant Body is our spiritual warrior aspect; if it is strong, we can face our lives with great courage and see them as a series of opportunities and adventures rather than as a succession of difficulties and stress. When the radiant body is strong, we have more than enough courage, strength and endurance to keep going and be successful in the face of any challenge time and space throws at us.

An uplifted spirit is the Radiant body quality that allows us to come through anything brilliantly and cheerfully no matter what setbacks, obstacles or challenges we face. Practicing this set enhances our radiance so that we don't give up when prosperity is right around the corner. It strengthens the aura and sciatic nerve.

I find it helpful as you inhale, to visualize taking in the energy in the form of light, a luminous white light. During the pause in breathing, give the energy the time and space it needs to spread within you and become transformed. During exhalation, let that expended energy flow back out of you. With every breath, there is more light and clarity in your physical, mental, and emotional realms.

Start in **Easy Pose.** Bring your arms up with your elbows bent. Keep the upper arms parallel to the floor and the forearms perpendicular to the floor. Bend your wrists so that your palms are flat facing upwards, fingers pointing out. Concentrate on the Third Eye point (with your eyes closed, direct them towards the spot midway between your eyebrows), and do long deep breathing for 1–3 minutes.

Hear the mantra Sat Nam with every breath. Sat Nam means, "I am truth" and, with this mantra, connect to your inner truth…feel radiant as you breathe.

Remain in Easy Pose: inhale, and as you exhale, bring your hands to the center of your chest (**Prayer Pose**). Concentrate on the third eye and do long deep breathing for 1–3 minutes. I find it helpful to continue to hear the sound Sat Nam and see a beautiful light around myself, to feel beautiful, joyful, and peaceful on each breath; now inhale and hold the breath as you draw the navel in; press the palms together firmly. Exhale.

Sufi grinds–place your hands with palms down on your knees; begin circling your torso from the base in one direction, keeping your spine straight. Feel the maximum stretch at the heart level. Inhale as you rotate forward; exhale as you rotate back. Change direction halfway through. Continue 1–3 minutes. To end, inhale, come back to the center, straighten the spine and apply root lock by pulling in your navel and pulling in and up on your anal sphincter; exhale and relax. I find that moving faster produces more heat at the base of the spine.

Cow Pose–Get on your hands and knees, as though you are a table, with your hands under your shoulders and your knees under your hips, all parallel; press your belly down, lift your heart, draw your navel in and up, lift your tail bone, lift your left leg and reach back with your right hand, grab your left foot and use the strength of your leg to open up the shoulder, draw the navel in and up; begin Breath of Fire (a quick inhale and exhale through the nose, with the emphasis on the exhale); continue for 1–3 minutes then switch legs and arms and repeat for 1–3 minutes. (I would suggest that if you cannot grab your foot, take hold of your pants leg or just bring your arm back by your foot.)

Backwards Pose or Reverse Table Pose–(Bridge Pose for Kundalini yogis) Sit with your legs bent and your feet flat on the floor, shoulder width apart. Place your hands on the floor behind you with your fingers pointing away from your body. Inhale and raise your hips until they are in a straight line with the upper body and thighs. Exhale and lower your hips down to the original position. Keep your chin parallel to the floor in both positions. Continue this movement between postures, inhaling up and exhaling down for 1–3 minutes. Afterwards, shake your arms and legs out.

Balance Standing Pose–Come to a standing position, and stretch your arms above your head in a Prayer Pose. Balance poses are all about focus; I find it helpful to begin by concentrating on my left foot, spreading my toes and pressing down the 4 corners, my little and big toe and both the left and right sides of my heel; then I inhale, drawing my tailbone under and engaging my navel. Give this a try, and remember not to be rigid: allow ease in your posture; bend forward from your hips as you aim your right leg back and your arms straight ahead; stare and be steady. (I would suggest that if you need to touch a wall to hold the pose, do so.) Take long deep breaths. Stay for 1–3 minutes. Do not repeat with your left leg.

Crow Squats–Feet are shoulder width apart; exhale as you squat down and bring your arms straight overhead, touching your palms together. Inhale and come back to a standing position, releasing your arms to your sides. Continue this motion as if you are fanning yourself between postures with deep breathing for 1–3 minutes. Hear Sat Nam w/ every breath.

Lie down on your back, and, keeping your feet together and flexed, raise your legs to 90 degrees; raise your arms so they are parallel to your legs; make sure your palms are facing each other. Hold with long deep breathing for 1–3 minutes.

Bring your legs down for savasana or **Corpse Pose**, and if you wish, relax on your back for 3–5 minutes before moving into the next meditation.

Meditation to Develop the Radiant Body–Sit in Easy Pose. With your fingers interlocked in-between your palms and your palms facing the ground, lift your hands over your head with your thumbs extending to the back. Tuck your chin and pull your arms back and slightly down until they are directly over the back of your neck. Chant any version of Ajai Alai with or without music (5 minutes).

Imagine yourself as you are—radiant, strong, fearless—your heart is lifted, your navel is back.

Ajai Alai is a powerful mantra chanted during the meditation that can lift you out of depression and anger. About it, Yogi Bhajan said, "Whenever you are in trouble mentally or you are being attacked in one way or another chant these words and opposition will dissolve in your face". Written by Guru Gobind Singh, the 10th Sikh Guru, these powerful words are an ode to the Divine.

Pronunciation	Translation
Ajai Alai	Invincible, Indestructible
Abhai Abai	Fearless, Unchanging
Abhoo Ajoo	Unformed, Unborn
Anaas Akaas	Imperishable, Etheric
Agunj Abhung	Unbreakable, Impenetrable
Aluck Abhuck	Unseen, Unaffected
Akaal Dayaal	Undying, Merciful
Alake Abhake	Indescribable, Uncostumed
Anaam Äkaam	Nameless, Desireless
Agaahaa Adhaahaa	Unfathomable, Incorruptible
Anaatay Paramaatay	Unmastered, Destroyer
Ajonee Amonee	Beyond Birth, Beyond Silence
Naraagay Narangay	Beyond Love, Beyond Color,
Na Roopay Na Raykay	Beyond Form, Beyond Shape
Akaramang Abharamang	Beyond Karma, Beyond Doubt
Aganjay Alaykhay	Unconquerable, Indescribable

Opportunity & Green Energy or Kriya for 4th chakra

I am including this set because it was the first kriya or yoga movements that I did when the idea for the book came to me. Several sources have done excellent jobs of describing this kriya, so I refer you to either *Yoga for Prosperity* by Siri Kirpal Kaur Khalsa, page 90, or page 85 of *The Kundalini Yoga Experience* by Dharam S Khalsa and Darryl O'Keefe.

The practice of this prosperity set opens the heart chakra and stimulates the crown chakra. This makes it possible for us to attract those opportunities that are in harmony with our souls.

Set for Opportunity and Green Energy images can be found at the back of the book.

4
Your Own Experience! Journal Pages

*As a single footstep will not make a path on the earth,
so a single thought will not make a pathway in the mind.
To make a deep physical path, we walk again and again.
To make a deep mental path, we must think over and over
the kind of thoughts we wish to dominate our lives.*
–Henry David Thoreau

I have included pages for every single day for 41 days. On days 1, 2, 11, 22, 40, and 41, I have suggested specific questions that you might want to reflect upon. You may write freely on the other blank pages. Use the space as necessary and as you see fit to do so.

Writing is a discipline. This particular practice allows you to free your mind, to release the thoughts "that disturb your being" and open yourself to quiet, so you can watch, allow, breathe, and "Be".

I would encourage you to go within to nurture self-awareness and the ability to reflect on your relationship to this technology and your Self. It can be powerful.

A dear friend and fellow teacher, Derek Amarpreet Whitman shared with me his essay on the benefits of keeping a yoga journal. As I believe his thoughts encapsulate the power of journaling, I am sharing his essay with you in its entirety:

Keeping a yoga journal is an important part of expanding my awareness during my Kundalini yoga practice. By writing down my intentions for each practice, and logging my yoga and meditation experiences, I hope to identify wanted and unwanted thinking and behaviors. I want to get the most out of the time that I devote to my daily practice, and I want to be able to recognize when I am making progress or getting the results that I seek.

Some of the reasons why keeping a yoga journal is an effective tool:

Meditation and yoga releases emotions. A yoga journal helps me process feelings so that I don't carry around worry, fear, anger, or resentment. The terrific thing about meditation is that I am processing difficult emotions on my time rather than throughout the day when I'm trying to focus on other things. My yoga journal is a good place to process things that have been bothering me. Now that I've identified uncomfortable emotions during meditation, I can purge those feelings and release them onto paper. Later, if those subjects still bother me, I have my journal to refer to as I confer with someone else about them.

I want something to help me continue my practice during times when I am not very motivated. My yoga journal helps me identify what I'm grateful for so that I may keep a positive perspective during challenging times. It is much easier to quit than to keep up, and by identifying what I appreciate, I avoid falling into a trap of getting discouraged when I don't recognize results fast enough.

Your Own Experience!

Writing in my yoga journal helps build accountability. When there is something that bothers me, there is always something wrong with me—not others. My yoga journal helps me identify what my role is in every life experience.

A yoga journal assists me in identifying the habits that block me. Deeper still, I can learn to discover the causes and conditions that manifest my habits, and then I have the choice to keep the habits I want, and discard the habits that no longer help me to become the person that I want to become.

Journaling helps me identify and reinforce the progress that I make and to set goals. This is probably the clearest way to recognize my forward progress, since I can literally turn back pages in my yoga journal to find out what I was thinking, feeling, and doing at any point in time.

Whether I write in my yoga journal upon awakening, after sadhana, before meditation or following meditation, or any time something good happens, I am identifying, solidifying, reinforcing, and purging my experiences for a more happy, healthful present.

Day 1

Write here the name of the kriya or meditation you are choosing and what motivated you to choose/do this one. (i.e. were you feeling lost or anxious, or were you needing a change in your financial or emotional state or needing more exercise in your life?)

Name of Kriya or meditation:

Time/Length of meditation:

I chose this because:

Your Own Experience!

My Intention or goal is:

Day 2

The chakra or chakras that I am stimulating is/are (Reference Chakra addendum if necessary):

The balance of this Chakra within me is:

Your Own Experience!

The unbalanced side of this chakra relates to my:

Experience of first 2 days has been:

Day 3

Your Own Experience!

Day 4

Day 5

Your Own Experience!

Day 6

Day 7

Your Own Experience!

Day 8

Day 9

Day 10

Day 11

A day of reflection and inspiration.

How are you doing? Keeping up? What are your feelings? Are there changes in your life? Perhaps you might want to review parts of the kriya to make sure the reasons/explanations given in the instructions are still in line with your intention. Check in with your intention.

I feel…

My energy level has (risen or fallen):

Your Own Experience!

I have noticed these changes:

If doing a Kundalini kriya – the best and most difficult parts are:

My intention (from Day 1) remains the same? I would like to add?

Biggest challenge so far in doing this (remembering to do it, time/length of meditation or kriya, what has come forward in my life around the intention):

Your Own Experience!

Day 12

Day 13

Your Own Experience!

Day 14

Day 15

Your Own Experience!

Day 16

Day 17

Your Own Experience!

Day 18

Day 19

Day 20

Day 21

Day 22

High spiritual number and Master number of revelation.
I am one with the Universe.

Any changes? Energized? Spacey?

Do I want to increase or decrease the minutes if I began the meditation or yoga for less than the suggested time?

Changes I have felt and noticed:

Others have noticed this about me:

Your Own Experience!

Effects on my physical body are:

Today is a day to give freely of my abilities and resources. I can do this by:

Day 23

Your Own Experience!

Day 24

Day 25

Your Own Experience!

Day 26

Day 27

Your Own Experience!

Day 28

Day 29

Your Own Experience!

Day 30

Day 31

Your Own Experience!

Day 32

Day 33

Your Own Experience!

Day 34

Day 35

Your Own Experience!

Day 36

Day 37

Your Own Experience!

Day 38

Day 39

Your Own Experience!

Day 40!

Completion! Time to regroup and decide if you should continue on to 90 days or change your meditation or kriya.

Will I rest for a week or longer?

Or will I continue?

Why?

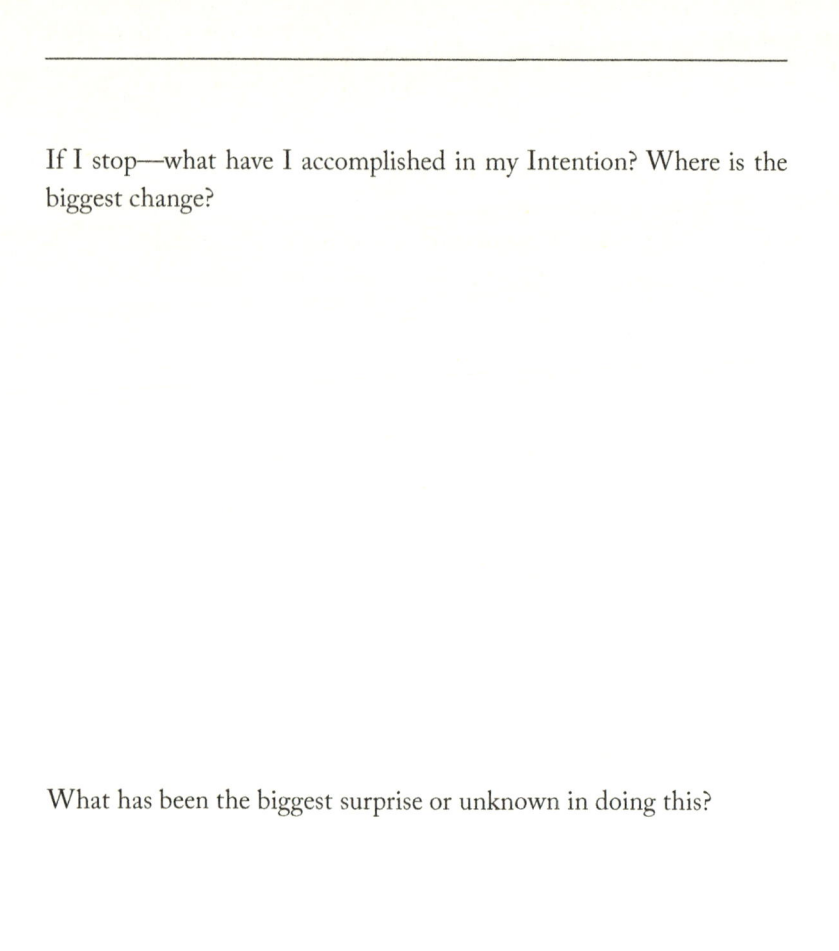

If I stop—what have I accomplished in my Intention? Where is the biggest change?

What has been the biggest surprise or unknown in doing this?

Your Own Experience!

Has this discipline deepened my commitment and changed my character?

Day 41

If you did not continue – how do you feel without doing it?

This is the day after, and I sense within myself (emptiness, completion, etc.):

Allow thoughts to flow and jot down any words that come up (anything at all pertaining to your life in any way).

Let your mind go as you take a colored pencil or other marker and express your Experience!

5
What to do After 40 days?

Resolve to be radiant
Keep Up!

My first response is that you can continue, if you like, up to 90 or even 1000 days.

Or you could decide to make a change and begin a new meditation or kriya or both.

And lastly, you could choose to rest for a period and see where your intuition takes you.

I have certainly done all of the above.

Though it is ultimately your choice whether you continue with this practice, I would like to leave you with some thoughts about discovering the value of making sadhana or a 40-day commitment an integral and continuing part of your life.

A friend sent me the following e-mail about the importance of awareness in his life:

"I've heard it said that traveling the Spiritual Path (a conscious journey, as opposed to moving through life without awareness) is like walking a razor's edge: we need to be open and totally surrendered (without ego: "gentle," if you will) enough to be perceptive, and yet we need to make use of a dynamic and powerful ego in order to be able to push through hard circumstances."

He continues, "For myself, I think people do whatever they do and call it what they will. I just like to feel the energy flow. I feel like the Light is always ON. Part of me is always at peace, while part of me reacts to the daily crises and agitations that happen (at work, for example) with heightened adrenalin and disturbed demeanor. Anyway, I think any Spiritual practice is good, bears positive fruit, and usually leads to more, and so, Spiritual growth."

That powerful ego my friend mentions maintains the course we set through a 40-day practice. And if it is tempered, refined and aids us in making choices, we can then keep that neutral meditative space in all we do, not just when we are sitting at home in a pleasant environment with no distractions.

My Spirit is accustomed to a routine of 40 or 90 days, a practice I began when I participated in my 1st Summer Solstice in New Mexico almost 6 years ago. I feel lost without a ritual of this sort to set my compass each day. And also, there are so many beautiful chants to sing and a multitude of kriyas to choose from to help me live at my best.

What to do After 40 Days?

Feeling the energy flow—yes! It is a treat to do sadhana for me. A delicious savory food that I imbibe each morning before the sun rises.

The sadhana keeps me flowing and open, which means I agree to look within and challenge myself not only to keep seeking peace, but to see that I am peace—Ong So Hung*.

---

*Ong So Hung–word in Gurmuki meaning "I am at Peace."

6
Pitfalls & Tips on how to avoid them for beginners, experienced practitioners, and vacationers

*"When the time is on you, start, and
the pressure will be off."*
(Bhajan 6)

The problem with beginning any new routine is that as soon as you say to your mind, I'm doing this for X amount of time, all the forces will come down to agitate. Trust the science of 40 days and know nothing will be given to you to ruin your life. This time can be very challenging. Many changes occur, and some people cannot finish. That's okay.

Yogi Bhajan has said, "Your discipline cannot be rigid. Your discipline is self-acknowledging, and you need to go along with it." Having a rigid mindset going into this, such as thinking, "I *will* do this. I have to do this in order to…" and/or becoming obsessive with getting to the end, is not a yogic attitude and will not serve you as much as doing what you can and blessing what you have accomplished if it doesn't work out to finish the meditation. The days you did do it served you well. However, some yogis say to follow through and finish no matter what, and if your personality is such that you cannot peacefully let something go, you may choose to follow these yogis' advice. Commitment and flexibility are central to practicing meditation or following through on any change in your life. Here are some ideas to help you get started and follow through with your 40 days. Though many are directed at beginners, it never hurts experienced practitioners to remind themselves of what they already know. After all, conscious, positive repetition is the key to all change.

Before you start
- Know it will change your sleep pattern.

- Set up a support network with friends or family. (Facebook or another social networking site might work for some, but not for others; find a way to get support that works for you.)

- Try to make it easier on yourself by indulging in a better diet. This time can be very challenging, and your body will adjust more easily if it does not have to deal with toxins.

- Make a commitment to yourself to follow through, but also an agreement not to beat yourself up for times that you do not.

Picking a 40-Day Practice
- Begin easy.

- Pay attention to one thing.

- Get comfortable with the often-uncomfortable idea of self-devotion. All things start with self-love. It's as if you picked up your iPhone and dialed in your Soul. Start talking things out; open up contractions that are blocking you.

- Start by blessing yourself every night for 40 nights when you are lying down. Tell yourself what you love about you because you will be blessing your essential self—the Soul. "I am a yogi. I am a good cook. I help plants grow." This will be a gesture of hugging yourself psychically.

- Start out with something fun.

- Start out by creatively eliminating a habit you'd like to stop. For example, many of us repeatedly use phrases, indicating and insidiously reinforcing self-doubt or lack of self-worth such as "You know what I mean?" or "I'm sorry." As we all know, repetition is destiny. Pick a phrase that you would like to stop saying, and tell yourself you will no longer say that phrase. Agree to fork over a quarter or $1, if you are prosperous, every time you say it.

- If you don't know what to start with, ask your teacher to help you choose what to do.

Staying on the path
- Be creative!

- Keep your friends and family involved in helping you keep your intention, through Facebook or any medium that works for you.

- Don't judge yourself harshly or compare yourself to others. "Sat Nam" means where you are at is where you are at; you are perfect where you are; focus on where your truth brings you. Congratulate yourself for finding your place and experience your truth.

- If you fall out of your routine, don't feel guilty; instead, make it your intention to try again.

- Make your mind responsive to who you are.

- Be really flexible. This practice can be demanding or delightful depending on your attitude. A good meditation will break your old patterns, put in a seed for a new pattern, and clear out the subconscious. Remember, all discipline begins with long deep breathing.

Logistical issues

- If you miss a day, and you have just started, then it is probably best to begin again. (See Mehtab's suggestions in 40 Ways for 40 Days.)

- In some instances, if necessary, you can split your practice up and do it in several pieces throughout the day, but it depends on what you are doing. If you are practicing a certain kriya, then you complete the whole exercise each time. I have done a number of repetitions of a mantra throughout the day. Just make sure to complete it in a 24 hour time period (i.e. So Purkh).

- If you are having trouble starting at the recommended duration of 11 or 31 minutes, do it for as long you can and feel good about it. If 1–3 minutes is all you can do, great, but, if you can, continue to increase until you have reached the time given.

- If you do not like the one you started with, it is best to continue with it anyway. I have experienced that situation and worked through my block. The purpose of the task at hand is to build strength and to work the change that you've chosen. Keep up.

- If you discover you have been doing the meditation/kriya in the wrong way, it is best to begin anew. What is your gut saying to you? Of course, it is always your choice; however the cells begin to change the memory every so many days—you want to get to the right circuitry as soon as you can.

- If you are looking for new meditations or kriyas, in addition to the ones I have included in chapter 3, there are references and websites listed at the end of this journal.

- Don't get hung up on whether or not you notice a change right away. Don't judge the experience—just "listen". How does it serve you to judge it, to qualify it, to measure it? Wait; have patience.

What to do if you are traveling or guests are staying with you

Making time: Whether you are staying with someone else or you have a guest in your home, prepare your family or friends ahead of time, before the actual visit, so that they can ask questions and "get" that this is very important.

Making Space

If you are flying: In the plane, do whatever mantra you have chosen silently with eyes closed, and, if you can, sit in Easy Pose or some comfortable seated posture with your spine lengthened. Visualize in your mind the hands in a position (mudra) if this part is awkward and there is no room to do so (i.e. Sat Kriya). Or, plan to do your meditation during a layover. Many airports now have meditation/quiet rooms to do yoga and the like—inquire before your trip to prepare.

If you are a guest at someone else's house: Get up early and find a nice park or take a yoga class nearby and arrive early to do your routine. I would be as up front and as gracious as possible with your friend or family member, and it will happen. There's always a way.

If you have guests at your house: use another room for your meditation; adapt, go outside to a quiet and perhaps secluded space. Ask your friends or family for ideas; tell them you get up early and need quiet for X amount of minutes.

Staying Healthy

Regarding your diet when traveling—keep it light to have enough energy and strength to get by on a different schedule. Remember to include some protein with every meal and that all grains become sugar in the body—perhaps stick with quinoa and amaranth, as these are higher in fiber and protein than other grains. Allow your body plenty of rest.

Making exceptions

I experienced letting go of a meditation when my boys came to visit for 10 days. I had begun two meditations several days before they came, and that was fine until we got busy. It just was not possible to actually accomplish everything that I wanted to do and rest wholly, have fun and work while they were here so I said to myself, "It's ok, no guilt—move on."

Missing Days

40 days without a break is the rule because it is only after 40 consecutive days you will experience the desired impact. So, if you miss a day, you can continue and still gain benefits; there is no loss in this, but if you

wish to achieve the full benefits of completing a 40-day practice, you must start again. Keep this in mind when you read the following:

40 Ways to Do 40 Days
By Mehtab, Founder of Yoga Yoga studios in Austin, Texas

And while we all may begin this life-changing journey with enthusiasm, there will be bumps along the way.

1. Start today.
2. Mark off days on a calendar.
3. Set up a daily email reminder on your computer.
4. Make a note card that says "Yoga" and put it on your pillow after you get up.
5. Get someone to be your 40-day yoga practice friend.
6. Make another positive change in your life at the same time (diet, exercise, etc.).
7. Create a routine, same time every day.
8. Reward yourself at the end of each week.
9. Talk about it (Facebook it!) so people will ask you how you are doing with it.
10. Read an inspiring book over the 40 days.
11. Visualize what you will be like after 40 days and write it down.
12. Write in a journal everyday.
13. Keep it fresh, vary the setting.
14. Do it especially when you are traveling or away from home.
15. If you get sick, spend the time visualizing that you are doing your yoga.
16. Be realistic; set a small goal you know you can reach and then exceed it.

17. Know you will hit a wall and be prepared to climb over it.
18. Watch for how your mind will try to trick you.
19. Be grateful.
20. Take the results into the real world.
21. All excuses are self-abuses.
22. Inspire someone else to do it.
23. Put a note in your car or on your computer– remind yourself of your higher self.
24. If you miss one day, never miss the next day.
25. If you miss one day, do it twice the next day.
26. If you miss one day, add a day.
27. If you miss one day, do another 40 days.
28. Document your avoidance behavior.
29. Take a picture of yourself after every week—before and after 40 days!
30. Remember why you did this in the first place.
31. Pray.
32. Laugh.
33. Remember it's okay to feel bad when you are trying to be better.
34. Never negotiate with your mind—command it.
35. Not having the time is not acceptable.
36. Idiots think—saints do.
37. Keep up and you will be kept up.
38. Think about your next 40 days.
39. The victory in life comes from winning the small battles.
40. Don't stop.

Appendix A: Chakras

The chakras are energy systems flowing through the body.

Seven correspond to nerve plexuses in the body and the 8th is associated with an auric field surrounding the body.

The first three are referred to as the lower triangle and the 5th, 6th and 7th as the upper triangle, with the 4th acting as a point of balance between them.

Opening and balancing the chakras is a main purpose of Kundalini yoga as they affect our thoughts and energy on all levels. They are one way to make sense of life.

Think of the chakras as lotus flowers, beginning life in the mud but reaching toward the sun to open, in this case, each one opening towards our inner light, helping us become aware of our life's purpose and our own individual characteristics as we grow towards the light within. Each spinning wheel of the chakras relates to certain body parts, which correspond to energies that we can activate more or less. "In addition, they transform the frequencies into sensations that the human being understands: thinking and feeling" (Hirschi 204). Awareness and becoming conscious activate the Radiance of the Soul to grow and glow.

The 1st chakra, located at the base of the spine, relates to the earth element and represents the mind and emotions when we are most unconscious. It has to do with our habits and instinct for survival. Being safe is the main focus of this chakra (whether or not you have a home over your head, food on your table, money in your bank account, and a job to make these things possible, as well as how you go about achieving these things all relate to the first chakra). A well-balanced 1st chakra allows you to be vulnerable and present in the moment as well as trusting in the Infinite source and valuing yourself. An unbalanced one can result in addictive behavior and avoidance of intimacy, as well as workaholism. The Sat Kriya provides balance for the 1st chakra.

The second chakra is associated with water. It is located in our pelvic area. Water relates to movement and change, and this chakra is concerned with feelings, desires, and passion. A person with a strong second chakra energy aligns with their emotions and enjoys fulfilling relationships. If this chakra is well developed, you have genuine closeness. An overactive or under active second chakra may lead to viewing the world through sex and/ or having shallow relationships. This can lead to addiction as well. Exercises to help balance and stimulate this chakra are Frog Pose and Sat Kriya.

Fire is the element associated with the **3rd chakra** at the navel point and is the area of will power and a sense of coordination. This is the power and projection zone. Kundalini energy is initiated and begun near the navel point. The energy lotus for this chakra represents completion. By keeping the 3rd strong, you organize the lower 3 chakras to make inroads to the upper realms of consciousness. An unbalanced 3rd leads to greed and an attitude of "what's in it for me?" Equilibrium here allows you to attain control over your life and awareness of the effects of your actions. Poses known to work for this chakra are Stretch Pose, Sat Kriya and Archer.

The fourth chakra represents the heart area and the air element. This is where spiritual awareness integrates with physical experience. This spot has to do with feelings (loving someone and compassion), as well as giving and accepting wholly and completely with happiness. The heart is what enables us to filter our different relationships. "Hum" is the sound used to stimulate this chakra. Any blocks to breathing affect this center, so pranayama or breathing exercises are good. An unbalanced fourth can lead to grief and loneliness, whereas with an unblocked 4th, you have unconditional love for all.

The 5th chakra or throat area is associated with the thyroid and parathyroid glands. The element is ether. Sat Nam is spoken here—Truth! This is where we work on speaking and teaching and knowing how to project. Purification is our purpose; communication, the focus; and mantra and the vibration of sound, our tools. Balance allows you to be able to express yourself and be in the present moment. Mantra is the tool for this chakra.

The 6th, 7th and 8th chakras represent vastness and being in our higher centers. All meditation strengthens these.

Intuition or opening an inner light is the focus of working on your 6th chakra. This is awareness—knowing within and perceiving so that you make correct choices and do not let your imagination run away with your thoughts. If the 6th is low in it's vibrational level in your body, you might not trust your intuition.

Seventh or crown chakra is associated with perception and an awakening of the Infinite. All meditation is to help open this area. In the 7th we are all One. Here is where we understand that aloneness means one with Source. If this chakra is operating too much in your life, you could be over-analyzing your actions.

The 8th is the aura surrounding the physical body and acts as a shell surrounding the other chakras. It relates to the body's electromagnetic field. If this aura is strong, and the other chakras are functioning well, your desires and needs are effortless.

An easy way to remember the chakras:

Root–I am safe.

Belly–I feel.

Navel–I act in awareness.

Heart–I love with compassion.

Throat–I speak my truth.

Third eye–I see.

Crown–I know.

Appendix B:
Explanation of Meditation Duration

KY Meditation Days
According to Yogic science, the human mind works in cycles. We can use the various cycles to replace unwanted patterns of behavior with new, more positive ones:

40 days of meditation will embody new experiences or increased competence and abilities.

90 days of meditation will clear our subconscious and build new habits.

120 days of meditation will allow our subconscious to realize awareness of the change in our daily lives.

1000 days of meditation will allow us to experience self-mastery and confirm our consciousness beyond every change of time, space and circumstance. A 1000-day practice projects our newfound awareness, mastery and consciousness impersonally for all. (It is impersonally personal, a discipline of grace that blesses all.) In mythical and symbolic traditions like numerology, the number 1000 represents the nobility of the individual.

KY Meditation Minutes

Yogic science says that there are specific lengths of time needed for certain desired effects during meditation. Most meditations are done for 11 or 31 minutes.

3 minutes of meditation affects the electromagnetic field and the circulation and stability of the blood.

11 minutes of meditation begins to change the nervous and glandular systems.

22 minutes of meditation balances the three minds, and they begin to work together.

31 minutes of meditation allows the glands, breath, and concentration to affect all the cells and rhythms of the body. It lets the psyche of the meditation affect the 3 *gunas (this refers to the 3 conditions of matter— Sattvic or pure, Rajasic or active, and Tamasic or decay, inertia)*, all 31 *tattvas (elements such as earth, air, water, ether, and fire)*, and all layers of the mind's projections.

62 minutes of meditation changes the gray matter in the brain. The subconscious "shadow mind" and the outer projection are integrated.

Appendix B: Explanation of Meditation

2-1/2 hours of meditation changes the psyche in its co-relation with the surrounding magnetic field so that the subconscious mind is held firmly in the new pattern by the surrounding universal mind.

Appendix C:
Where to Find Meditations and Yoga Exercises Mentioned in Chapter 2

So Purkh Meditation can be found on pages 93-98 in: Khalsa, Shakti Parwha Kaur. *Marriage on the Spiritual Path.* Kundalini Research, 2007. Print.

Burn Inner Anger can be found on page 147 in: *Praana Praanee Praanayam: Exploring the Breath Technology of Kundalini Yoga as Taught by Yogi Bhajan.* Kundalini Research Institute, 2006. Print.

Meditation for Projection & Protection for the Heart can be found on page 437 in: Bhajan, Yogi, Ph.D. *The Aquarian Teacher: KRI International Teacher Training in Kundalini Yoga as taught by Yogi*

Bhajan; Level 1 Instructor. Fourth Edition. Santa Cruz, NM: Kundalini Research Institute, 2007. Print. And online at www.shaktakaur.com

Guru Ram Das Rhythmic Harmony for Happiness
can be found on page 157 in: Khalsa, Gurucharan S. *Kundalini Yoga: Sadhanna Guidelines, 2nd Ed.* Santa Cruz, NM: Kundalini Research Institute, 2007. Print.

Indra Nittri Meditation
can be found on page 424 in: Bhajan, Yogi, Ph.D. *The Aquarian Teacher: KRI International Teacher Training in Kundalini Yoga as taught by Yogi Bhajan; Level 1 Instructor*. Fourth Edition. Santa Cruz, NM: Kundalini Research Institute, 2007. Print.

Sat Kriya Workout
can be found on page 379 in: Bhajan, Yogi, Ph.D. *The Aquarian Teacher: KRI International Teacher Training in Kundalini Yoga as taught by Yogi Bhajan; Level 1 Instructor*. Fourth Edition. Santa Cruz, NM: Kundalini Research Institute, 2007. Print And online at http://www.pinklotus.org/-%20KY%20Kriya%20for%20Sat%20Kriya%20Workout.htm

Meditation to Break the Mask
can be found in: *Transformation – Volume One: Mastering the Self. (Seeds of Change for the Aquarian Age Vol.1)*. Santa Cruz, NM: Kundalini Research Institute, 2010. Print.

Meditation to Tap Opportunities
can be found on page 68 in: Khalsa, Siri Kirpal Kaur. *Yoga for Prosperity*. Yogi Ji P, 2002. Print.

Green Energy Kriya or Kriya for the 4th Chakra
can be found on page 85 in: Khalsa, Guru Dharam S. and Darryl O'Keefe. *The Kundalini Yoga Experience: Bringing Body, Mind, and Spirit Together*. Touchstone, 2002. Print.

Vipassana or Mindfulness Meditation can be found in: Hart, William. *The Art of Living: Vipassana Meditation as Taught* by S.N.Goenka. HarperOne, 1987. Print.

Kriya to Balance and Recharge the Nervous and Immune System can be found in: Khalsa, Gururattan Kaur and Ann Marie Maxwell. *Transitions to a Heart Centered World: Through Kundalini Yoga and Meditations of Yogi Bhajan*. Yoga Technology P, 1988. Print.

And in: Khalsa, Gururattan Kaur and Guru Rattana. *Relax and Renew: with Kundalini Yoga and Meditations of Yogi Bhajan*. Yoga Technology P, 1988. Print.

Deep Memory of a Past Projection can be found on page 165 in: Bhajan, Yogi and Gurucharan Singh. *The Mind*. Espanola, NM: Kundalini Research Institute, 1998. Print.

Bound Lotus can be found in: Kaur, Mahan Kirn. *The Bound Lotus Manual*. Print. And online at www.mahboundlotus.com

25th pauri (Bahuta Karam) of Japji Sahib and **Kirtan Sohila or "Song of Peace"** can be found in: Doabia, Harbans Singh. *Sacred Nitnem*. 26 Ed. Amritsar, India: Singh Brothers, 2004. Print.

Subagh Kriya can be found on page 132 in: Khalsa, Shakta Kaur. *Kundalini* Yoga. DK Adult, 2000. Print.

Appendix D: Resources

Books
Bhajan, Yogi, Ph.D. *The Aquarian Teacher: KRI International Teacher Training in Kundalini Yoga as taught by Yogi Bhajan; Level 1 Instructor.* Fourth Ed. Santa Cruz, NM: Kundalini Research Institute, 2007. Print.

Hirschi, Gertrude. *Mudras: Yoga in Your Hands.* York Beach, ME: Red Wheel-Weiser, 2000. Print.

Khalsa, Gurucharan Singh. **Kundalini Sadhana Guidelines**. 2nd Ed. Santa Fe, NM: Kundalini Research Institute, 2007. Print. Filled with Meditations and Kriyas

Khalsa, Guru Dharam S. and Darryl O'Keefe. *The Kundalini Yoga Experience: Bringing Body, Mind, and Spirit Together.* NY: Fireside-Simon and Schuster, 2002. Print.

Khalsa, Shakta Kaur. *Yoga for Women.* DK adult, 2007. Print.

Khalsa, Siri Kirpal Kaur. *Yoga for Prosperity.* Yogi Ji Press, 2002. Print.

Saraswati, Swami Satyananda. *Asana Pranayama Mudra Bandha.* 4th Ed. Munger, India: Bihar School of Yoga, 2008. Print.

Websites

Yogic Tools for Chronic & Critical Illness (yogic-tools.com) This is a place to go to for more information on Guruatma, one of the presenters in this book. She offers a unique perspective on yoga for people with disabilities, but is also a consultant and yoga therapist.

Kundalini Yoga (www.kundaliniyoga.org) Free online courses and more information on the chakras.

Reiki For Holistic Health (reiki-for-holistic-health.com) Chakras

Kundalini Research Institute (kundaliniresearchinstitute.org) Access to the teachings of Yogi Bhajan

Kundalini Rising (www.kundalinirising.org/kykriyas.html) More meditations and yoga exercises to choose from when preparing your 40 days.

A View on Buddhism (viewonbuddhism.org/Meditations/basic_meditation.html) Basic Buddhist meditations

Pinklotus (pinklotus.org) Kundalini yoga sets and meditations

Kathe Forrest & Keep the Change (keepthechangenow.com)
The website for this book as well as class schedules and upcoming workshops

Spirit Voyage (spiritvoyage.com) Music from around the world and a link to the global 40-day sadhana

DVDS
Radiant Health with Naam Yoga by Joseph Michael Levry—This DVD explains quite well the Ra Ma Da Sa chant for healing and includes over 32 mudras for imbalances such as weight loss, mental clarity, nerve strength, sluggish digestion and more.

Works Cited

"5 Basic Teachings." Unity of the Valley. Url: http://www.unityofthevalley.org/topmenupages/whatisunity/5basicteachings.html. 2011. Web.

Bhajan, Yogi, Ph.D. *The Aquarian Teacher: KRI International Teacher Training in Kundalini Yoga as taught by Yogi Bhajan; Level 1 Instructor*. Fourth Ed. Santa Cruz, NM: Kundalini Research Institute, 2007. Print.

Bhajan, Yogi. Lecture. Espanola, NM, 7/26/90.

Bhajan, Yogi and Gurucharan Singh. *The Mind*. Espanola, NM: Kundalini Research Institute, 1998. Print.

"Change." Dictionary.com. Url: (http://dictionary.reference.com/browse/change). Web.

Hine, Emily. "40 Days of Meditation and Yoga." *HineSights*. Url: http://Emilyhine.com. February 24, 2010. Web.

Hirschi, Gertrude. *Mudras: Yoga in Your Hands*. York Beach, ME: Red Wheel-Weiser, 2000. Print.

Kaur, Snatam and Ganga Bhajan Kaur and Livtar Singh Kaur. *"Kabir's Song."* www.snatamkaur.com

Khalsa, Guru Dharam S. and Darryl O'Keefe. *The Kundalini Yoga Experience: Bringing Body, Mind, and Spirit Together*. NY: Fireside-Simon and Schuster, 2002. Print.

Khalsa, Gurucharon Singh, Ph.D. "Meditations for an Invincible Spirit in the Aquarian Age." Kundalini Research Institute. Url: (http://www.kundaliniresearchinstitute.org/100day). Web.

Khalsa, Siri Kirpal Kaur. *Yoga for Prosperity*. Yogi Ji Press, 2002. Print.

Life According to Yogi Bhajan.com. Url: (http://www.harisingh.com/newsYogiBhajanSays.htm) Web.

Rumi. Facebook https://www.facebook.com/#!/mevlana? Web.

"The Significance of the Number 40 in Islam." The Muslim Voice. Url:(http://themuslimvoice.wordpress.com/20 09/04/ 22/why-is-the-number-40-important-in-islam/). Web.

About the Author

Kathe Forrest grew up in a traditional Catholic family. In many ways, her life has followed the usual path: she has 3 children and has been married and divorced. However, the unusual has been a large part of her experience as well.

Since she was in her middle 20's, Kathe has lived in 12 states, traveled through 22, and visited Australia and Europe. At one time, she hiked the Continental divide, living in a tent for 2 months, until the snows came and forced her to decide to live in Idaho. Her path has led her into many professions; she has been a model, a co-op owner, the manager of a health food store, a laboratory technician, an astrologer, a librarian and a veterinary assistant, among other things. And all along her path, she has followed her heart and intuition, seeking her soul's desire. She began studying hatha yoga in college while attending the University of Houston. Subsequently, she studied the philosophy and ideas of many yogis including: Marcia Moore, Sivananda, Indra Devi, and Swami Vishnudevananda. In 1988, she began an intensive 10-year study in both hatha and Kundalini Yoga, during which time she took the spiritual name Siri Kirin, meaning "Great Ray of God's Light." She completed her Aquarian Trainer Level One Kundalini Teacher training through Yoga Yoga in Austin and is also certified in traditional hatha yoga. Studies in nutrition and alternative therapies have contributed to the scope of her understanding of the mind-body connection.

In addition to teaching through Brenham Community Ed for 7 years while also running her own yoga studio, she has taught at the 3HO Summer Solstice in New Mexico several times by invitation and has given workshops and classes on relationships, prosperity, the chakras, and moving through and into a more fulfilling life after age 40.

Her path has been and always will be yoga in some form, working towards freeing the self from its non-eternal elements. As she says, " It seems very natural to me to do yoga, meditate and be consistent with a practice. I gain wellness of the body, mind and spirit. I believe that we can all make a difference and change the destructive course the earth is on by shifting the planetary consciousness, becoming more aware each day. I feel that in writing this book/journal I become one more person acknowledging the practice and rewards of committing yourself to something for 40 days."

Kathe began writing this book in January 2012 and during the birth of this book has completed eleven yoga practices/ meditations, not only in order to appreciate the benefits of each one, but also to find strength and endurance and ideas for the writing. Below is the list of kriyas and meditations that she finished.

Kriyas/Meditations done while writing *The 40 Day Sadhana Companion*

1. Kriya for Green Energy or 4th Chakra, 40 days
2. Ganapati began New Years Eve, 11 days.
3. Meditation to Tap Opportunities, 120 days

4. Sat Kartar, 41 days

5. Poota Mata Kees Asees (chant), 40 days

6. Sat Guru Prasad/Ek Ong Kar with Spirit Voyage, 40 days

7. Tapa Yog Karam Kriya, 40 days

8. 35th Pauri recited, 40 days

9. Grace of God and Sat Kriya, 3 min each, 40 days

10. Basic Spinal Energy Series & Tattva Balance Beyond Stress and Duality, 40 days

11. Prosperity meditation, 40 days

Kathe can be reached through her website keepthechangenow.com.

My Story

My story of 40 days began when I attended my first Summer Solstice in 2007. It was different than anything that I had experienced in my life up to that point.

I was up earlier than I dreamed that I could be up in the morning. I sat in the wee hours of the dawn singing and praying and bowing and loving it.

This went on for 10 days. At the end of the next to last day or perhaps last day – one of the teachers, Guru Singh, gathered us together for a final farewell and inspirational talk. He suggested to find a partner and to be in touch over the next 40 days as you begin this practice with the purpose of "keeping up". Anandjot (Michael Orzen) and I decided to join forces and do this together. Over the next 40 days we called and talked about how we were doing, ways to improve our spiritual habits and difficulties we had encountered in ourselves on returning home and discovering others around us were not as enlightened. (This is a joke, of course!) We were sadhana companions for almost 5 years and believe me it was well worth the effort. We became good friends, led and taught joint classes at Summer Solstice and in Oregon and the friendship deepened because of our 40 days times 4 years' worth of discipline.

Radiant Kriya

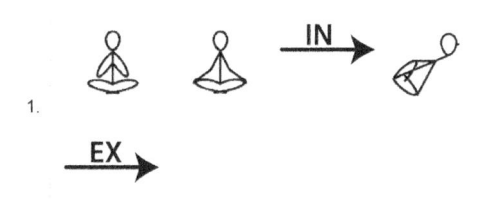

1. Begin in Easy Pose. Long deep breathing for 1-3 minutes.
Sufi Grinds - circle around the base of your torso.

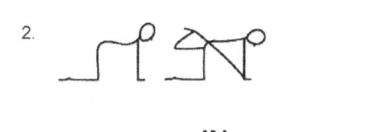

2. Cow pose - reach back to left leg with right arm and begin Breath of Fire - 1-3 minutes and switch legs and arms

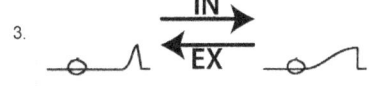

3. Reverse table Pose/Bridge Pose

4. Stretch your hands above your head in prayer pose. Bend forward from the hips as you aim the right leg back and arms straight ahead. Take long deep breaths.

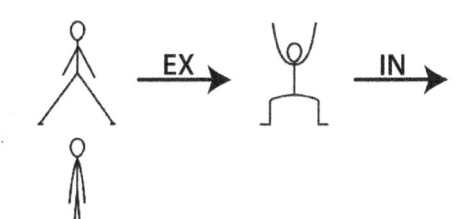

5. Exhale as you squat down and bring palms together. Inhale, come back to standing, releasing arms to the side

6. Raise the legs to 90 and with feet flexed raise arms to parallel legs. Palms are facing each other. LDB 1-3 minutes

7.		Corpse pose
8.		Fingers interlocked in-between palms and palms facing the ground, lift hands over your head with thumbs facing back. Chant any version of Ajai Alai.

Set for Opportunity and Green Energy

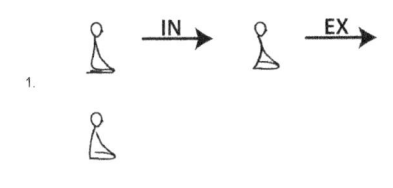

1. **Spinal flexes**
Inhale flex the spine forward while mentally chanting Sat and focus at the base of the spine. Exhale and flex back. Inhale Sat Exhale Nam Head stays level, Continue 2-3 minutes.

   Sit on heels with hands on thighs.
   At the end of the time - inhale with spine straight. Hold the breath out 10 secs.

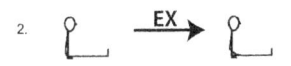

2. **Body Drops** - Hands on ground by hips - lift the body up by pushing down with your hands and then drop.
Continue 3-5 minutes

3. **Crow pose**
Squat down, feet flat if you can. Place arms out in front in Ksepana mudra. Hold position and begin BOF*. 2-3 minutes. To finish - Inhale and project from the heart.

   Mudra - Fingers interlaced and index fingers extended, thumbs cross one another.
   * Breath of Fire*

4. **Run in place** - bring knees up high and punching out with alternate fists.
Continue 3-5 minutes.

5. **Kundalini Lotus** - Hold big toes or ankles, balance on the buttocks, keeping back, legs and arms straight.
Hold position with Breath of Fire 2-3 minutes and then Inhale and draw the energy up the spine.

6. Sitting on left heel, place right foot on left thigh. Cup the hands at naval and chant Ong So Hung - focus is on the heart chakra.
No time set.

7. Extend the arms out from easy pose and focus on sending energy from one palm to the other - arch overhead from left palm to right.

8. Easy pose with hands in Venus Lock behind the neck. Begin to bow forward as you exhale Nam, inhale up while mentally chanting Sat. Continue 2-3 minutes.

9. Easy pose, place the arms straight out in front with palms down. Inhale and raise right arm up 60 degrees. Exhale and lower it. Then repeat with left arm. the pace is rapid.

10.
A. Hands in Venus lock above the head with palms facing down.
B. Change hands to index fingers up
C. Move all fingertips to form a teepee

A. Begin BOF and energy projects out top of the head.
B. Focus is the same only LDB - Long Deep Breathing
C. Same focus - BOF Inhale, hold the breath, project out the top of the head. Exhale and relax.

11. Relax arms by the side and palms are flat and facing forward. Visualize green energy and chant
Haree Haree Haree Har - Chant 2-11 minutes and then rest hands on knees in Gyan mudra. Meditate on all your blessings.

Gyan Mudra - Thumb and index fingers touching.

Made in the USA
Las Vegas, NV
05 April 2025